Published by Nona Books in 2022

First edition; First printing

Illustrations and design © 2022 Nona Books

Printed in the United States of America

www.nonabooks.com

coloring the true colors of BIRDS

from the author

Hello dear readers,

I'm so excited to share my latest project with you - a coloring book featuring some of the most beautiful birds from around the world! As an avid birdwatcher and artist, I've always been captivated by the stunning diversity of these feathered creatures, and I wanted to create a way for others to appreciate their beauty as well.

In this book, you'll find illustrations of backyard birds like the Barn Swallow and the Hummingbird, exotic birds like the Atlantic Canary and the Kookaburra, water birds like the Crane and the Swan, and forest birds like the Peacock and the colorful Woodpecker. Each page includes a short description of the bird, along with its true colors to help you color your illustrations as accurately as possible.

I've also included a colored image of each bird on the back cover of the book, so you can reference it as you color. My hope is that by bringing these birds to life through art, you'll gain a deeper appreciation for their unique characteristics and the incredible diversity of the natural world.

Coloring is not only a relaxing and meditative activity, but it's also a wonderful way to connect with nature and learn about different species of birds. I've poured my heart and soul into this project, and I hope that it brings you as much joy and inspiration as it has brought me.

Thank you for joining me on this journey, and happy coloring!

Sincerely,
Iris.

P.S. - I would love to hear your feedback, questions, or suggestions about this book. Please feel free to reach out to me at **iris@nonakid.com** - I can't wait to hear what you think!

Coloring Tips

We hope that you enjoy coloring the birds in this book as much as we enjoyed creating them. To make your coloring experience even more enjoyable, we have put together some coloring tips to help you get the most out of this book.

Firstly, we have printed each illustration on a single-sided page to reduce the bleed-through to the following image. This means you can use a variety of coloring tools without worrying about ruining the next page. We recommend using colored pencils, markers, gel pens, or watercolor pencils to bring your magical houses to life.

If you decide to use markers, we recommend placing a piece of cardstock or thick paper behind the page you are working on. This will help prevent the ink from bleeding through and staining the next page. It's always best to test your markers on a small section of the page before coloring the entire image to ensure that you like the way they look.

Another important tip is to take breaks and stretch your hands and wrists periodically. Coloring can be a relaxing and therapeutic activity, but it can also strain your hands and cause cramping. So, take breaks, stretch your hands, and give your eyes a rest.

Finally, whether you color alone or with friends, relax, get your creativity out and enjoy your art. There are no rules or expectations, just have fun and let your imagination run wild. If you're looking for inspiration, you can try experimenting with different color combinations, adding your own details, or even creating a story for the house you're coloring.
Thank you for choosing this coloring book of magical houses. We hope that these tips help you make the most of your coloring experience.

Happy coloring!

Iris.

color test page

this book belongs to:

_____

_____

Table of Contents

Table of Contents (cont.)

Birds of Prey

Parrots

Ground-Living Birds

Northern Cardinal

The Northern Cardinal is a popular sight to see around birdfeeders in the winter months. The Northern Cardinal was named for the male's red crest which is reminiscent of a Catholic cardinal's red cap. Found throughout all areas where there are thickets or heavy bush. Expanding farther north every year and this is credited to the outdoor feeder stations being put out in the winter months. Seen from Nova Scotia to the south of the Canadian borders into the central USA, down into Arizona to the southern tip of Florida. It is the official bird of seven eastern U.S. states and is especially common in the Southeast.

Males are bright red with a black mask and an orange beak. Females are duller red or brown.

Barn Swallow

The barn swallow is found in Europe, Asia, Africa, and the Americas. It is a bird of open country that normally uses man-made structures to breed and consequently has spread with human expansion.

This species lives in close association with humans, and its insect-eating habits mean that it is tolerated by humans. The preferred habitat of the barn swallow is open country with low vegetation, such as pasture, meadows, and farmland, preferably with nearby water. This swallow avoids heavily wooded or precipitous areas and densely built-up locations.

In literature, it is often referred to as a symbol of spring or summer, and it is one of the most depicted birds on postage stamps around the world.

The barn swallow has steel blue upperparts and a reddish-brown forehead, chin, and throat, separated from the off-white underparts by a broad dark blue breast band. There is a line of white spots across the outer end of the upper tail.

5

Gouldian Finch

The Gouldian finch is a colorful passerine bird that is native to Australia and was exported worldwide. During the breeding season, they are normally found on rough scree slopes where vegetation is sparse. In the dry season, they will move to wherever their food and water can be found.

They are easily caught by predators due to their beautiful colors. When a male is courting a female, he bobs about and ruffles his feathers in an attempt to show off his bright colors. He will expand his chest and fluff out the feathers on his forehead.

It has been shown that female Gouldian finches from Northern Australia can control the sex of their offspring by choosing mates according to their head color.

Their plumage is purple, gold, green, blue, and black. Their face may be red, orange, or black.

European Greenfinch

The European Greenfinch is widespread throughout Europe, North Africa and Southwest Asia, and has also been introduced into Australia, New Zealand, Uruguay, and Argentina. It has been seen in North America, but because they are known as captive and cage-raised finches, they are not recognized as wild birds in North America. They are thought to be escaped birds.

This bird can be found in woodland edges, farmland hedges, and gardens with relatively thick vegetation that are favored for breeding. It nests in trees or bushes.

It is yellow on the wings and tail.

The English poet William Wordsworth wrote a poem about this species entitled 'The Green Linnet' in 1803.

Blue Jay

The blue jay is native to eastern North America and occurs in southern Canada and throughout the eastern and central United States.

The Blue Jay is a brightly colored large blue bird common around birdfeeders, especially, if nuts or sunflower seeds are being offered. It is known as a noisemaker, sounding off alarm calls to warn intruders.

The blue jay occupies a variety of habitats, from the pine woods of Florida to the spruce-fir forests of northern Ontario. It is less abundant in denser forests, preferring mixed woodlands with oaks and beeches. It has expertly adapted to human activity, occurring in parks and residential areas.

Its plumage is lavender-blue to mid-blue in the crest, back, wings, and tail, and its face is white. The underside is off-white and the neck is collared with black which extends to the sides of the head. The wing primaries and tail are strongly barred with black, sky-blue, and white. The bill, legs, and eyes are all black. 22

Kingfisher

Kingfisher is a small to medium-sized bird with a cosmopolitan distribution, with most species found in the tropical regions of Africa, Asia, and Oceania but also can be seen in Europe. The typical kingfishers are river dwellers and can be found in deep forests near calm ponds and small rivers.

The kingfishers have excellent vision, they are capable of binocular vision and are thought to have good color vision.

Kingfishers are generally shy birds, but in spite of this, they feature heavily in human culture, generally due to the large head supporting their mighty mouth, their bright plumage, or some species' interesting behavior.

This handsome crested bird flies off over the water when disturbed, uttering a loud rattling call. It is bluish gray above and across the breast and white below. The females have a brownish red band or "belt" across the lower breast.

26

House Sparrow

House Sparrow is a small bird found in most parts of the world. It is strongly associated with human habitation and can live in urban or rural settings. Though found in widely varied habitats and climates, it typically avoids extensive woodlands, grasslands, and deserts away from human development.

The house sparrow is well adapted to living around humans, it frequently lives and even breeds indoors, especially in factories, warehouses, and zoos.

The plumage is mostly different shades of grey and brown. The female is mostly yellow-brown above and below, while the male has boldly colored head markings, a reddish back, and grey underparts. The underparts are pale grey or white, as are the cheeks, ear coverts, and stripes at the base of the head. The upper back and mantle are a warm brown, with broad black streaks, while the lower back, rump, and upper tail coverts are greyish brown.

Hummingbird

Most of the hummingbird species are native to North America. They are the smallest-sized bird species in all of the bird families living on the continent.

Hummingbirds live in many types of landscapes, which consistently include an abundance of flowers. Their name is derived from the prominent humming sound their wingbeats make while flying and hovering to interact with other birds. These colorful birds pique the curiosity of all who see them.

They are specialized for feeding on flower nectar, but they also consume insects or spiders. Hummingbirds are specialized pollinators and thus their bill length, bill shape, and body mass are correlated with the structure of the flowers.

To serve courtship and territorial competition, many male hummingbirds have plumage with bright, varied coloration. By merely shifting position, the feathers of a muted-looking bird can instantly become fiery red or vivid green.

Magpie

There are Magpies found in temperate regions of Europe, Asia, and western North America. The birds called 'magpies' in Australia are, however, not related to the magpies in the rest of the world.

Magpies are widely considered to be intelligent creatures. The Eurasian magpie, for instance, is ranked among the world's most intelligent creatures and is one of the few non-mammal species able to recognize itself in a mirror test. They are particularly well known for their songs and were once popular as cage birds.

The best-known species often called the black-billed magpie (Pica pica), is a black-and-white bird, with an iridescent blue-green tail.

American Crow

The range of the American crow now extends from the Pacific Ocean to the Atlantic Ocean in Canada, on the French islands of Saint-Pierre and Miquelon, south through the United States, and into northern Mexico.

The crows are scavengers and eat a wide range of foods. They are known for their cunning ways and are perceived as intelligent and adaptable to human environments. They are wary of man because he is their main predator. These birds will not tolerate any type of birds of prey and will taunt and attack them until they leave their territories.

The American crow is a large, distinctive bird with black feathers all over. Its legs, feet, and bill are also black. The most usual call is a loud, short, and rapid caaw-caaw-caaw. American crows can also produce a wide variety of sounds and sometimes mimic noises made by other animals, including other birds such as barred owls.

Mourning Dove

The Mourning Dove is the common wild pigeon of North America. It is identified by its long pointy tail and wings and what appears to be a small head. This dove is a regular visitor to the backyard feeders and is seen feeding both on the ground under bird feeders or on platform feeders, where it has a proper footing. It prefers open country and is not a forest bird. It is considered a game bird in many US states. Even though it is harvested in the high millions every year, its population does not seem threatened. It is protected in other states and in Canada and preserved as a songbird.

The plumage is generally light gray-brown and lighter and pinkish below. The wings have black spotting, and the outer tail feathers are white, contrasting with the black inners. Below the eye is a distinctive crescent-shaped area of dark feathers. The eyes are dark, with light skin surrounding them.

Eurasian Hoopoe

The Eurasian hoopoe is widespread in Europe, Asia, and North Africa, and northern Sub-Saharan Africa.

The hoopoe can be found in two types of habitat: bare or lightly vegetated ground and vertical surfaces with cavities (such as trees, cliffs, or even walls, nest boxes, haystacks, and abandoned burrows).

Its call is a soft "oop-oop-oop", which may be the explanation for the bird's name. An alternative explanation is the French name of the bird, huppée, which means crested.

It is a distinctive cinnamon-colored bird with black and white wings, a tall erectile crest, a broad white band across a black tail, and a long narrow downcurved bill.

It spends most of the time on the ground probing for grubs and insects.

In the Torah, hoopoes were listed among the animals that are detestable and should not be eaten.

Atlantic Canary

The Atlantic Canary is a small passerine bird native to the Canary Islands, the Azores, and Madeira. It occurs in a wide variety of habitats from pine and laurel forests to sand dunes. It is most common in semiopen areas with small trees such as orchards and copses. It frequently occurs in man-made habitats such as parks and gardens.

The bird is named after the Canary Islands, not the other way around.

The color 'canary yellow' is in turn named after the yellow domestic canary, produced by a mutation that suppressed the melanins of the original dull greenish wild Atlantic canary color.

The male has a largely yellow-green head and underparts with a yellower forehead and face. The lower belly and under-tail are whitish and there are some dark streaks on the sides. The upper parts are grey-green with dark streaks and the rump is dull yellow.

Kookaburra

Kookaburras are native to Australia and New Guinea. The name is derived from 'guuguubarra' in Wiradjuri (the traditional language of the Wiradjuri people of Australia), which sounds like its call. The loud, distinctive call of the laughing kookaburra is widely used as a stock sound effect in situations that involve an Australian bush setting or tropical jungle, especially in older movies.

They are found in habitats ranging from humid forest to arid savannah, as well as in suburban areas with tall trees or near running water. Though they belong to the larger group known as "kingfishers", kookaburras are not closely associated with water.

This is a woodland-dwelling bird with gray and brown plumage.

Also sometimes called the "bushman's clock," the kookaburra is heard very early in the morning and just after sunset.

Rhinoceros Hornbill

The rhinoceros hornbill is a large bird living in forest trees. In captivity, it can live for up to 35 years. It is found in lowland and mountain, tropical and subtropical climates, and in mountain rain forests in Borneo, Sumatra, Java, the Malay Peninsula, Singapore, and southern Thailand.

The courtship and bonding of these birds are critical, as the female must trust the male to provide her with everything when she is incubating and raising chicks. These hornbills make their nests inside tree trunks, and the female stays inside with the eggs and then with the chicks, while the male brings them food.

The plumage is mainly black, with white legs and a white tail with a black band. The huge bill and casque are orange and red. The eyes of the male are red with black rims, and white with red rims in the female.

77

Woodpecker

The woodpeckers are found worldwide, except in Australia, New Guinea, New Zealand, Madagascar, and Antarctica. They occur in forests or woodland habitats, mainly in tropical rainforests.

Woodpeckers have strong bills that they use for drilling and drumming on trees, and long, sticky tongues for extracting food. The bill's chisel-like tip is kept sharp by the pecking action of birds that regularly use it on wood. The pecking causes the woodpecker's skull to heat up, which is part of the reason why they often peck in short bursts with brief breaks in between, giving the head some time to cool.

In some species, the plumage is patterned in black, white, and red, and many have a crest or tufted feathers on their crowns. Pileated woodpeckers are mainly black with a red crest and have a white line down the sides of the throat.

81

Peacock

Male peafowl is referred to as peacocks, and female peafowl are referred to as peahens, even though peafowl of either sex are often referred to colloquially as "peacocks".

A peacock's copulation success rate depends on the colors of his eyespots (ocelli) and the angle at which they are displayed.

The angle at which the ocelli are displayed during courtship is more important in a peahen's choice of males than train size or the number of ocelli. Actions such as train rattling and wing shaking also kept the peahens' attention.

Peafowls are forest birds that nest on the ground, but roost in trees.

The Indian peacock has iridescent blue and green plumage, mostly metallic blue and green, but the green peacock has green and bronze body feathers. The peacock tail consists not of tail quill feathers, but highly elongated upper tail coverts. These feathers are marked with eyespots, best seen when a peacock fans his tail.

Toucan

Toucans are native to the Neotropics, from Southern Mexico, through Central America, into South America south to northern Argentina. They mostly live in the lowland tropics. The toucans are forest species and are restricted to primary forests.

The wings are small, as they are forest-dwelling birds who only need to travel short distances

Toucans make a variety of sounds. The very name of the bird (from the Tupi language of Brazil) refers to its predominant frog-like croaking call, but toucans also make barking and growling sounds. They also use their bills to make tapping and clattering sounds.

The most common Toucan is mainly black with lemon yellow on the face, throat, and chest, bright red under the tail, and multicoloured markings on the bill.

Crane

The crane is a very large bird with long legs and a long neck with a worldwide distribution except in South America.

Superficially, cranes resemble herons but usually are larger and have a partly naked head, a heavier bill, more compact plumage, and an elevated hind toe. Many species of cranes are dependent on wetlands and grasslands, and most species nest in shallow wetlands. These birds, much like swans, fly with straight necks, as opposed to herons who fly with their necks curled back to their bodies. The cranes are much more vocal than swans or herons and their bugling can be heard for miles around.

Cranes in open wetlands tend to have more white in their plumage than do species in smaller wetlands or forests, which tend to be more grey.

Penguin

Penguins are water birds that through evolution lost the ability to fly. They live almost exclusively in the Southern Hemisphere. They spend roughly half of their lives on land and the other half on the sea. Penguins are highly adapted for life in the water. Their wings have evolved to become flippers, useless for flight in the air. In the water, however, penguins are astonishingly agile. Penguins' swimming looks very similar to a bird's flight in the air. Most penguins feed on fish which they catch with their bills and swallow whole while swimming.

Most are black on the back and white below, often with lines of black across the upper breast or spots of white on the head. Colour is rare, being limited to red or yellow irises of the eye in some species. A few species have red beaks or feet, others have yellow brow tufts or orange and yellow on the head, neck, and breast.

Penguins have no special fear of humans, probably because penguins have no land predators.

105

Swan

Swans are among the largest flying birds. They are usually found in the Northern Hemisphere, North America, Australia, New Zealand, the Chatham Islands, and southern South America. Swans feed in water and on land.

Swans famously mate for life, although "divorce" sometimes occurs, particularly following nesting failure, and if a mate dies.

Although birds do not have teeth, swans have beaks with serrated edges that look like small jagged 'teeth' which are used for catching and eating their food.

Some species have pure white plumage, but others are mixed black and white. The Australian black swan is completely black except for the white flight feathers on its wings, and the light grey chicks. The South American black-necked swan has a white body with a black neck. The swan legs are normally a dark blackish grey color, except for the South American black-necked swan, which has pink legs. The bill may be black with yellow for some species while it's patterned red and black for others.

109

Seagull

Gulls, or Seagulls, are seabirds with a worldwide distribution. They are more adept at walking on land than most other seabirds. They breed on every continent, including the margins of Antarctica and the high Arctic. Gull species may breed and feed in marine, freshwater, or terrestrial habitats.

Gulls are resourceful, inquisitive, and intelligent, the larger species in particular. They demonstrate complex methods of communication and a highly developed social structure. For example, many gull colonies display mobbing behavior, attacking and harassing predators and other intruders.

The general pattern of the plumage is a white body with darker wingtips that varies from pale grey to black, with white markings. The ivory gull is entirely white, while other species are partly or entirely grey.

American Flamingo

The American Flamingo is a large wading bird that was once called the Greater Flamingo and is considered part of the flamingos from the West Indies and Mexico. It is the only flamingo that naturally inhabits North America. Usually found in flocks in shallow, saline lagoons. Flamingoes fly in straggling lines, much like geese, and their honking and braying calls can also sound rather like geese.

The flamingo is using its long legs and large webbed feet to wade and stir up the bottom of the water bed to bring up its food.

The American flamingo has reddish-pink plumage. The wing coverts are red, and the primary and secondary flight feathers are black. The bill is pink and white with an extensive black tip. The legs are entirely pink. The call is a goose-like honking.

Gray Heron

The Grey Heron is a long-legged wading bird of the heron family, native throughout Europe and Asia and also parts of Africa. it can be found anywhere with suitable shallow watery habitat that can supply its food. the Grey Heron is a large bird with has a long neck retracted, and has a slow flight.

They have a white head and neck with a broad black stripe that extends from the eye to the black crest. The body and wings are grey above and the underparts are greyish-white, with some black on the flanks. The long, sharply pointed beak is pinkish-yellow and the legs are brown.

The plumage is largely ashy-grey above, and greyish-white below with some black on the flanks.

123

Puffin

The puffins are stocky, short-winged, and short-tailed birds. These are seabirds that feed primarily by diving in the open seawater. They are found in the North Pacific Ocean and the North Atlantic Ocean. Their short wings are adapted for swimming with a flying technique underwater. In the air, they beat their wings rapidly in swift flight, often flying low over the ocean's surface.

The colorful outer part of the bill is shed after the breeding season, revealing a smaller and duller true bill beneath. Because of their striking appearance, they are also referred to as "clowns of the sea" and "sea parrots".

The common puffin is black above, and white below, with gray face plumage, red-orange feet, and a blue-gray, yellow, and red bill.

Pelican

Pelicans are found on all continents except Antarctica, mainly in warm regions. They are very large water birds with very long bills and inhabit inland and coastal waters such as lakes, rivers, and seacoasts in many parts of the world. They feed mainly on fish, catching them at or near the water surface by using the extensible throat pouch as a dip-net. The pouch is not used to store the fish, which are swallowed immediately.

Pelicans swim well with their strong legs and their webbed feet. They rub the backs of their heads on their preen glands to pick up an oily secretion, which they transfer to their plumage to waterproof it.

the American white pelican has almost entirely white plumage, except for the black flight feathers, which are hardly visible except in flight. The breast is yellowish. The bill and the bare skin around the eye, and the feet have vivid orange color. Other Pelican species are either brown, grey or white.

131

Budgie Parrot

The budgerigar, also known as the common parakeet or shell parakeet, is a small, long-tailed, seed-eating parrot usually nicknamed the 'budgie' or in American English, the parakeet.

The little budgie bird is one of the most popular pets in the world, ranking just behind dogs and cats, and it's no wonder. This affectionate, cute bird is small and inexpensive, and if trained properly a budgie can mimic human speech. Budgerigars are about seven and a half inches long and come in hundreds of brilliant shades of greens and yellows. Generally, budgies are found in warm regions, from India to Australia and tropical America.

Naturally, the species is green and yellow with black, scalloped markings on the nape, back, and wings. Budgies in captivity have the coloring of blues, whites, yellows, greys, and even with small crests.

Macaw Parrot

Macaws are native to Central America and North America, South America, and formerly the Caribbean. Most species are associated with forests, especially rainforests, but others prefer woodland or savannah-like habitats.

The majority of macaws are now endangered in the wild and a few are extinct. The greatest problems threatening the macaw population are the rapid rate of deforestation and illegal trapping for the bird trade.

Macaws and their feathers have attracted the attention of people throughout history. Macaw feathers were highly desired for their bright colors and acquired through hunting and trade.

Its brilliant red, yellow, and blue plumage contrasts with a bare white face that may blush when the bird is excited.

141

Ara Parrot

The Ara macaws are large striking parrots with long tails, long narrow wings and vividly colored plumage. The name is from ará meaning "macaw" in the Tupi language of Brazil. The word is phonetically similar to the sound of their call.

The Ara macaws have a Neotropical distribution from Mexico to Argentina. The Ara macaws are generally fairly adaptable in their habitat requirements. The only requirement is sufficient large trees, which is where they obtain their food and breeding holes.

The colors in the plumage of the Ara macaws are spectacular. Some species are predominantly green, two species are mostly blue and yellow, and others are mostly red.

Galah Cockatoo

Cockatoos are found in Australia as well as in New Guinea and the Solomon Islands. Australia's commonest cockatoo is the Galah, also known as the rose-breasted cockatoo. Because of their bold and loud behavior, many are caged as pets. In captivity, cockatoos have a lifespan similar to humans. When tame, it can be an affectionate and friendly bird that can learn to talk, and mimic other sounds. While it is a noisy bird that may be unsuitable for apartment living, it is quieter than other cockatoo species. Like most parrots, the galah requires plenty of exercise and playtime out of its cage as well as daily social interaction with humans or other birds in order to thrive in captivity.

"Cockatoo" means 'grip' in Malay because of their incredibly strong beak. "Galah" means 'fool', 'clown' or 'idiot' in Australian slang.

The Galah has a pale silver to grey back, a pale grey rump, a pink face and breast, and a light pink mobile crest. It has a bone-colored beak and grey legs.

Bald Eagle

The bald eagle is the only eagle solely native to North America. It is the national bird of the United States. This magnificent bird is actually a sea eagle that can be seen throughout all of North America and commonly occurs inland along rivers and large lakes. The bald eagle typically requires old-growth and mature stands of coniferous or hardwood trees for perching, roosting, and nesting.

The bird is not actually bald, its name derives from its white-feathered head.
Both sexes are dark brown, with a white head and tail. The beak, eyes, and feet are yellow.

Owl

Owls are found on all continents except Antarctica and on most oceanic islands. The coloration of its plumage plays a key role in its ability to sit still and blend into the environment, making it nearly invisible to prey. Owls tend to mimic the coloration and sometimes the texture patterns of their surroundings.

Most owls are nocturnal, actively hunting their prey in darkness. Much of the owls' hunting strategy depends on stealth and surprise. Their eyesight and specialized hearing functions are particular characteristics of the owl that aids in nocturnal prey capture.

Their secretive habits, quiet flight, and haunting calls have made them the objects of superstition and even fear in many parts of the world.

Owls vary in color from white through many shades of tan, gray, brown, or reddish to deep brown. A few are solidly colored, but most are patterned with streaks, bars, or spots.

Eagle-Owl

The eagle owl is one of the largest species of owl and resides in much of Europe and Asia. Eagle-owls are found in many habitats, mostly in mountainous regions or other rocky areas, but also in coniferous forests, steppes, and other remote areas. They are often found in areas where cliffs and ravines are surrounded by a scattering of trees and bushes. The eagle owl is a nocturnal predator. At twilight, it perches on a branch while searching its territory for prey.

The eagle-owl is one of the longest-living owls on average, it can live for up to 20 years in the wild.

The eagle-owl is characterized by two tufts of feathers on the head and large orange eyes. The overall coloration is tawny, mottled with brown, lighter below.

Golden Eagle

The golden eagle is a bird of prey living in the Northern Hemisphere, it is present in Eurasia, North America, and North Africa. The golden eagle is a very large raptor. Golden eagles are sometimes considered the best fliers among eagles and perhaps among all raptorial birds. They are equipped with broad, long wings with somewhat finger-like indentations on the tips of the wing.

Despite the dramatic ways in which they attain food and interact with other raptors, the daily life of golden eagles is often rather boring. Adults were observed to sit awake on a perch or the nest for an average of 80% of the day.

These birds are dark brown, with lighter golden-brown plumage on their napes, golden lanceolate nape feathers, dark eyes, a gray and yellow beak, fully feathered legs, large yellow feet, and great talons.

Pheasant

Pheasants are heavy ground-living birds. Although they can be found all over the world, the pheasant's native range is restricted to Europe and Asia.

According to the Oxford English Dictionary, the word "pheasant" ultimately comes from 'Phasis', the ancient name of the Rioni River in Georgia.

The common pheasant, which is widespread throughout the world, can be found in wild areas and in farm operations. Various other pheasant species are popular in aviaries.

The Pheasant has a long brown-streaked black tail. The body plumage is bright gold or fiery copper-red and chestnut-brown plumage with an iridescent sheen of green and purple. The wing coverage is white or cream and black-barred markings are common on the tail. The head is bottle green and distinctive red wattle, and the neck has a white ring.

Wild Turkey

The turkey is a large bird native to North America and is associated with Thanksgiving. The reason why this bird shares the same name with the Republic of Turkey is probably a holdover from early shipping routes that passed through the country of Turkey on their way to delivering the birds to European markets.

Turkeys have been known to be aggressive toward humans and pets in residential areas. When they need to, Turkeys can swim by tucking their wings in close, spreading their tails, and kicking.

Despite its unwieldy appearance, Wild Turkey is a fast runner and strong short-distance flyer, with excellent vision and intelligent, wary nature that makes it an elusive quarry.

They have long reddish-yellow to grayish-green legs. The body feathers are generally blackish and dark, with areas of red, purple, green, copper, bronze, and gold. Males have a large, featherless, reddish head, red throat, and red wattles on the throat and neck. The wings are glossy bronze.

185

BIRDS TEACH A GREAT LIFE LESSON. ALL YOU HAVE TO DO IS LISTEN TO THEIR SONG.

About Nona Books

Welcome to our brand, where we believe in the power of the printed word to inspire, educate, and entertain. In a world filled with screens and constant distractions, it can be hard to find the time and space to truly connect with a good book. That's why we strive to create high-quality, engaging books for adults and kids alike, covering a wide range of genres and topics. From activity books that spark creativity and curiosity to guide books that provide practical advice and inspiration, we have something for everyone. Our goal is simple: to make books that stand the test of time and competition, and provide a respite from the noise of the modern world.

We hope you'll join us on this journey of discovery and enrichment through the written word.

Thank You!

Thank you for supporting us with your purchase! As a boutique publication, we have a small team and a limited budget. This may result in our book prices being higher compared to larger publications. But rest assured, our books are crafted with care and expertise, offering a unique blend of classic, educational, and entertaining content. Your support fuels our passion to continue creating top-notch books that provide an enriching and timeless reading experience.

Made in the USA
Las Vegas, NV
10 July 2023

74456027R00111